woodland adventure

☆ HANDBOOK ☆

Adam Dove

Frances Lincoln Limited
74–77 White Lion Street
London N1 9PF
www.franceslincoln.com

A catalogue record for this book is available from
the British Library.

978-0-7112-3713-1

Printed and bound in China

1 2 3 4 5 6 7 8 9

The adventures in this book have been led by a
qualified practitioner. They are a guide to inspire
adults in their work and play with children. It is
their responsibility to risk-assess all activities they
undertake, ensuring they are insured and first-aid
trained with all relevant qualifications and checks
completed and passed. Neither the authors nor
the publisher can accept any legal responsibility
for any harm, injury, damage, loss or prosecution
resulting from the use or misuse of the activities,
techniques, tools and advice in the book.
    It is illegal to carry out any of these activities on
private land without the owner's permission, and
you should obey all laws relating to the protection
of land, property, plants, birds and animals.

Designed by Jo Grey

Contents

Introduction

This book has been written to inspire parents, carers and teachers looking for ideas for children's activities using our most precious resource, nature. I am a champion of the Scandinavian model of early years education, where children spend most of their day playing outdoors, and for the past 10 years I have been involved in outdoor education as a qualified Forest Schools Leader. Here in the UK, Forest Schools are becoming increasingly popular because, as many studies show, children who participate in such programmes develop self-esteem, confidence and good social skills through positive experiences and self-directed learning.

I find the power of imagination and story telling make a huge impact on young children. What makes the adventures in my book so fun and rewarding is that they weave together activities with a story that allows the children to be involved with the final outcome.

The book is written in sections, like a recipe. First, read through the story to familiarise yourself with the adventure, then get things set up for the day following simple step-by-step instructions. There's no expensive equipment needed, most materials can be found around the home. Next, read the story to the children to outline what the adventure is about and what they need to do to complete it. 'Things to make' is the practical element, when the children create something like a wizards' wand or a journey stick. Everything links in to the theme of the session so the children aren't left wondering why they are doing something – they understand that there is a purpose behind it. Playing games that are linked to the adventure helps to develop key senses, such as hearing, touch, smell and sight, plus they are a great opportunity for the children to exercise and keep fit. Next comes tracking, which is when the children need to find their way through the woods to their end goal. Each trail is different and builds on new skills of stalking, observation, keeping quiet and listening attentively. At the end of the trail we find what it is we have been seeking, whether it's a fairy village, a fizzing volcano or a crock of gold. Finally, the group has a chance to reflect on what everyone has experienced during the day and the lessons learned.

There are no specific rules that have to be followed, only safety elements that one should always be aware off through risk assessment and common sense. Every group, for example, should include a trained first-aider. (Please also refer to the 'Keeping safe' pointers throughout the book.) You must also ensure you have the correct ratio of adult helpers to children: for two- to four-year-olds, that's one adult to every four children, for four- to eight-year-olds, one adult to every six children.

When I'm out in the woods with a group of children, I always establish an adventure call which I use each time I need to get their attention. Keep it simple and fun and introduce it at the start of the day. A favourite with the children I teach is, 'Oi! Oi!', to which they respond 'Eaaasy Tiger!' Works a treat.

Use your own imagination to bring the adventures alive in a personal way. If you feel inspired and enthused by what you are delivering, in turn, the children will have fun, too.

Adam Dove, 2015

Abracadabra! Wizards'

Improve hand-to-eye co-ordination through bark peeling and

magic colouring wands

learn how different colours blend together to create new ones

Telling the story

❝ *Hidden deep in the woods there is a tree with magic powers. It is said that just a drop of its sap can make colours swirl and dance before your eyes. Shall we see if we can find the tree and get a bottle of sap? We will have to sneak past the elf who guards it. Now, he may be very old and very short-sighted and have mislaid his glasses, but his hearing is excellent. He can hear a pin drop at 20 paces.* [Walk 20 steps and pretend to drop a pin – ask the children if anyone heard it.] *So, if we're to reach the tree, we must be very, very quiet and run as fast as the wind.*

There are two more things we need to make the magic work: we must follow a trail through the woods to find some colourful potions and we must make ourselves a wizard's wand. ❞

Setting up the adventure

You will need

Wizards' wands: dry and green wood sticks – see step 1 (for the best woods, see Keeping safe, page 19), cotton wool, hessian squares, rubber bands

Laying the trail: bottles of food colouring, green washing-up liquid, small travel-sized, plastic bottles, hessian squares, rubber bands, bag white flour, moss, leaves and grass, tree decorations, such as fake cobwebs, Green Man model, fairy doors

Things to make: gardening gloves, vegetable peelers, feathers, glitter glues, rubber bands, sticky tape

Games to play: blindfolds

Completing the adventure: water pistol, 1 litre (2 pints) full-fat milk, deep plastic bowls, plastic pipettes

1 Wizards' wands: one of the suggested children's activities in this adventure is bark peeling. The finished results look amazing, but there is a knack to it and you will have to show the children how it's done. (For how to do it, see page 14.). Note than green wood is easier to work than older, dry wood.

Top each stick with a small ball of cotton wool wrapped in hessian. **(a)** Secure with a rubber band. **(b)**

2 Laying the trail: wrap the bottles of food colouring (colour potions) in hessian and secure with rubber bands. Select a magic tree, then lay a trail of bottles running back to the children's play area. The bottles are very small, so tuck them alongside a path where the children will be able to find them. **(c)** A sprinkling of white flour (fairy dust) will help make them easier to find for very young children.

Decorate the magic tree with materials gathered in the woods, such as moss, leaves and grass, fake cobwebs, a Green Man and fairy doors **(i, p16)**.

Fill bottles with washing-up liquid (magic sap) **(d)** and hide them on the magic tree.

Things to make

☆ **Making wizards' wands:** first, show the children how to do bark peeling. Choose a stick (green wood is easier to work than dry), lay it flat on the floor or across your lap. Holding the top of the stick in your gloved hand, pull the vegetable peeler along the length of the stick. Work away from your hand. Once you get the hang of it you should be able to peel the bark off in long strips. Give each child a stick and a peeler and let them have a go themselves. Stripping the bark is just a decorative effect, so if some of them can't quite manage it, it doesn't matter. **(e)**

☆ **Decorating the wands:** once the children have finished peeling their sticks, they can decorate them with modelling clay, feathers, leaves, moss and grass. Use rubber bands, tape or sticky tape to fix the decorations in place. **(f)** Add a few dabs of glitter glue for a little extra magic.

Games to play

☆ **Getting to know trees game:** this is a fun way for children to learn to identify woodland trees and plants and develop their descriptive language. Older children can play in pairs; younger ones will need adult help. One child wears a blindfold and is guided to a tree by their partner. (Make sure they choose an accessible tree.) Using their hands, the blindfolded child feels the tree, noting the different textures and features, such as the bark. **(g)** Get them to describe what they are feeling with their fingers, eg, the rough bark or the soft, damp moss. If there's a distinctive knot on the trunk of the tree, get them to describe the size and shape of it. Their partner then walks them a few steps away from the tree and spins them round to disorientate them. The blindfold is removed then the child tries to find their tree. **(h)** Let each child play the game in turn.

Following the trail

☆ **Finding the magic tree:** tell the children that hidden along the path are bottles of colour potion (food colouring) that will lead them to the tree.

Completing the adventure

☆ **We've found the magic tree!** Line the children up in front of the tree and tell them that they must sneak past you to get to the bottles of magic sap (washing-up liquid) hidden near the fairy doors. If the children get squirted with water they must start their approach again. Sit next to the tree, pull on a blindfold and get ready with the water pistol. (You may need to explain why the elf has left you in charge of the tree today.) Doubtless, the children will want to play with the water pistol, too. **(i)**

☆ **Colour swirling:** for each child or group you will need a bowl of milk (stand it on a flat surface), a pipette, bottles of colour potion (food colouring) and a bottle of magic sap (washing-up liquid). Using a pipette, drip two drops of each food colouring on to the milk. **(j,k)** Squeeze some washing-up liquid on the hessian-covered tip of each wand. **(l)** Get the children to dip their wands in the bowls of milk. **(m)** Watch as the colours start to swirl.

ARE THE COLOURS MOVING AND CHANGING? HOW MANY CAN YOU SEE?

What did we learn today?

☆ How does it feel to be blindfolded? Was it fun or was it spooky?

☆ Can you think of any woodland creatures that don't need to look where they are going? Where do they live? (eg, moles and worms live underground)

☆ Where does sap come from? What can it be used for? (eg, glue, amber, rubber)

☆ Describe what tree bark feels like?

☆ Why should we look after trees?

☆ What can we use tree bark for? (eg, making paper, lighting a fire, making boats)

Keeping safe Willow and hazel are ideal woods for the children's sticks and for bark peeling. They can be coppiced (ie, having their branches trimmed regularly) without causing any harm to the tree. You might try asking a tree surgeon or gardening company if they have any prunings they might let you have. Most native tree wood is safe for children to handle but never use offcuts of laurel as it contains toxins.

'THE TREE BARK TICKLED MY FINGERS WHEN I TOUCHED IT'
MARCO

'I PUT GLITTER ON MY WAND TO MAKE THE MAGIC STRONGER'
ISLA

'I LIKED IT WHEN WE WERE PEELING BARK OFF THE STICKS'
YELDA

fairy and her unicorn?

provide opportunities for learning and great team work

Telling the story

❛ *Today I went to visit the fairy princess who looks after all the birds, animals, plants and trees in the woodland. But when I got to the magic tree where she lives, her neighbour the Green Man told me she'd gone out looking for her pet unicorn – a beautiful white horse with a silvery horn on its head that sends sparks flying every time it shakes its mane. The princess had heard her beloved pet whinnying down near the lake and had gone out to bring it home. But that was days ago...*

The dark waters of the lake are full of magic and danger and no one should go there on their own, not even a fairy princess. The Green Man said he thinks the princess may have sailed out to rescue her pet and been caught by a mysterious spell leaving her stranded in the middle of the lake. We must try to rescue them, but first we will need to build our own boats. ❜

will you help rescue a fairy and her unicorn?

Setting up the adventure

You will need

Princess' boat: hammer, U-shaped nail/staple, thick piece of bark, fairy and unicorn figurines, moss, leaves and grass for decoration, clear nylon fishing line, scissors

Laying the trail: bag white flour

Decorate the magic tree: fake cobwebs, fairy doors, Green man model

Things to make: bark, twigs, string, wooden skewers, bradawl

a

1 Make the princess' boat: hammer the U-shaped nail into the bark. **(a)** Position the figurines on top and decorate with moss, leaves and grass. **(b)** Attach the end of the nylon line to the U nail. **(c)** For the boat launch you need a stretch of still water. For the safety of the children, it should be easily accessible and where the water is shallow. Tie the end of the nylon line to a rock and cover it over with leaf litter or soil so the children can't see it. At the end of the game you gently tug the line to bring the fairy princess safely ashore.

2 Laying the trail: sprinkle a trail of flour (fairy dust) from your designated 'magic tree' to the water's edge. **(d)** For older children, you could lay a trail of stick arrows.

3 Decorate the magic tree: as well as lots of greenery, add fake cobwebs to give the fairy's home an abandoned look. **(e)**

25

Things to make

☆ **Building boats:** get the children to think about features their boat will need, such as a hull, sails and a mast. Stimulate their imaginations by showing them pictures of boats. For the hull, use a thick piece of bark or a handful of sticks tied together with string. Cover the deck with moss. Push wooden skewers into the bark for masts (use a bradawl to make holes in the wood first). Thread leaves on to the skewers for sails. **(f)** It's likely that you won't be able to retrieve the children's boats at the end of the day, so please use only natural, biodegradable materials that aren't harmful to pond life.

Games to play

☆ **The listening game:** to be able to hear the princess calling for help we must listen carefully. To help the children develop good listening skills and be aware of sounds around them, I get them to play a game devised by the American outdoor-educator Joseph Cornell. Ask them to be quiet, to close their eyes and hold up both hands in a fist. Each time they hear a sound they must put up a finger. **(g,h p28)** When they have used all their fingers ask them how many sounds they heard and what they think they were. Ask if there were any sounds they liked or disliked. Vary the game by getting them to raise a finger when they hear a bird or the wind.

Following the trail

☆ **Following the fairy dust:** the fairy leaves a trail of fairy dust (white flour) where she has walked. This is how we can track her. Get the children to test the fairy dust by touching it with a finger (watch they don't put it in their mouth). If it's the real thing they will feel it tingle – the power of suggestion should be enough to generate a tingle! If they don't, suggest it's because the princess has been lost for so long her dust has lost its magic. Quickly now, we will have to find her before all her magic is gone and she is stranded forever. Follow the trail to the water's edge.

Completing the adventure

☆ **Rescuing the fairy princess and her unicorn:** it's time for the children to launch their boats. They can help if it is safe to do so, but please be extra careful around water (see Keeping safe, page 31). Despite launching their boats the princess will probably remain stranded... so each group or child must cast a magic spell. Give a discreet tug on the nylon line attached to the princess' raft after each spell, gradually pulling her ashore. If the children's boats have sailed into the centre of the pond, be ready to tell them that their boats are needed to patrol the pond in case any other fairies get into difficulties. Quickly divert their attention to the rescued princess and her unicorn and celebrating her safe return home to the magic tree.

WATCH HOW THE WIND MOVES THE BOATS ACROSS THE WATER

What did we learn today?

☆ Why must we be careful around water?

☆ What can we use water for?

☆ What things in the forest float? What other things can you think of that float?

☆ What made the boats move across the water?

☆ What noises did you hear in the woods?

☆ Did you notice more when you were quiet and listening carefully?

Keeping safe Clear nylon fishing line is perfect for this adventure: it's virtually unbreakable and almost invisible. However, for young children, unsuspecting adults and wildlife there is a potential risk of entanglement – so use it carefully. For your boat launches, choose a stretch of water free of water birds and ensure the children are well supervised at all times. When water is involved in an adventure, you may consider having extra helpers on hand (see page 7 for ideal ratios of adult helpers to children). Before you start this adventure, talk to the group about the potential hazards and how best to keep everyone safe.

will you help rescue a fairy and her unicorn?

'MY BOAT GOT TO THE FAIRY PRINCESS AND THE UNICORN FIRST'
ELLIE

'I HEARD THE WIND MAKING THE TREES GO SCRATCH SCRATCH'
JOSH

'I HEARD A FROG GO GRRRUP, GRRRUP'
OSCAR

3 The woodland fairies

This multi-activity gets children working together in groups

and the big-footed troll

to learn basic woodcraft skills, tracking and how to build shelters

Telling the story

❝ *Once upon a time, deep in the woods, there was an enchanted village where the fairies and their friends the pixies, elves and tree spirits lived happily together. Each night, from sunset until sunrise, they would sing and dance and feast... until one day a troll came to the village, a troll so big that he made the trees look like matchsticks. Now, trolls may be gigantic but they are also very friendly and wouldn't dream of hurting a fly, but at the end of their long, long legs, they have enormous feet and sometimes their feet cause a lot of damage without the troll's head knowing anything about it. As he walked along, whistling and swinging his club, the troll's big feet squished and squashed all the fairies' houses and scared everyone away.*

This morning, though, there was a sign that the fairies might be returning home. There was some fairy dust near the entrance to the village near an old tree. Shall we welcome the fairies home by making them new houses? Until the fairies return home, though, we must ask the bog people to guard the village. Let's go and find them now. '

Setting up the adventure

You will need

Laying the trail: modelling clay, googly eyes (from craft suppliers), leaves, moss, pine cones

Water filters: fabric square/ clean sock, plastic cups, rubber bands, sand, moss, charcoal, plastic bottle of pond water

Fairy house: bark, sticks, fern fronds, pine cones, white flour

Things to make: modelling clay, googly eyes, gardening gloves

Games to play: hand-held drum

a

1 **Laying the trail:** make tree spirits. Press a ball of clay on to a tree trunk. Make a face using googly eyes, leaves for hair, a cone for a nose and moss for a beard. **(a)** Position tree spirits on at least five trees to make a good trail. Have each one face towards the next tree and the final one looking at the fairy village.

2 **Make water filters:** you may need to make up the filters for the younger children. For each filter, tuck the square of fabric (or the toe end of the sock) into the plastic cup and secure with a rubber band. Fill with layers of charcoal, moss and sand. **(b,c)**

Fill a bottle with pond water or mix a handful of mud and leaf debris into tap water.

3 **Make a fairy house:** use pieces of bark, sticks, fern fronds, moss, pine cones. Keep the design simple. **(d)** Sprinkle fairy dust (white flour) in the area.

setting up the adventure

Things to make

☆ **Making bog people:** give each child a lump of clay and a pair of googly eyes to make a bog person. Let them find other items from the forest, such as moss or feathers for hair, sticks for legs and arms, pine cone for a nose. **(e)** When collecting materials the children should wear gardening gloves to protect their hands.

Get the children to think about what their bog person will need to survive until the fairies return home, eg, food to eat, water to drink and to keep them warm and dry a campfire and a waterproof shelter.

☆ **Making water filters:** divide the children into groups, giving them the materials to make one water filter per group. **(f)** Once they have finished making their filter, pour in some dirty water and it leave to settle. Show the children the before and after results, holding the cups up to the light.

To get the children to think about food and water safety, ask them why the water in ponds, streams and rivers isn't safe to drink. Explain that although the filtered water they have just made is fine for the bog people and the fairies to drink, it wouldn't be safe for us. You could also ask them if we should eat food we find in the woods?

Games to play

☆ **The troll's drum game:** when the children hear the troll drum sound they must run as fast as they can and hide before the drum stops beating. **(g,h)** They must stay hidden and quiet until they hear you use your group's designated adventure call (see page 7), 'Oi! Oi!'. They in turn must shout out their response, 'Eaaasy Tiger!', before coming out of hiding.

Following the trail

☆ **Finding the fairy village:** divide the children into groups and let them take it in turns to find the tree spirits that lead the way to the fairy village. Tell the children to pay attention to the direction the tree spirits face and that the village will be marked by a sprinkling of fairy dust (white flour).

Completing the adventure

☆ **Rebuilding the village:** once the children have found the sprinkling of fairy dust (flour), show them the house you have made and tell them that the fairies need them to rebuild their village. Discuss what makes a good shelter, eg, a water-tight roof, a dry floor, walls. Collecting the materials to make the houses – branches, sticks, leaf litter, etc – and building are ideal group activities. Give the children gloves to protect their hands. **(i)**

Empty a watering can of water over each completed house to check for leaks; **(j)** if the ground underneath stays dry, a bog person can move in.

Ask the children what the bog person might find in the woods to eat. Go foraging together for berries, nuts and leaves and pile them up in the shelter. Don't forget the cup of filtered water. Take this opportunity to discuss the dangers of foraging: tell children never to eat or pick anything in the woods unless they are with an adult.

To extend this adventure over to the next time the children return to the woods, place a fairy figurine alongside each bog person and tell the children how pleased the fairies were to find their village rebuilt.

PRACTICAL AND
CREATIVE SKILLS COME
TOGETHER IN
THIS ACTIVITY

j

What did we learn today?

☆ What makes a good shelter?

☆ Did your fairy house keep out the water? If not, what materials could you use to make it more waterproof?

☆ What things do fairies and bog people need to live in the woods?

☆ Should we eat or drink things we find in the woods? If we did, what might happen?

☆ Why should we wear gloves during this adventure?

Keeping safe Discuss with the children the dangers of drinking dirty water and of eating things we find in the woods. If the children are very young it's best not to pick anything, such as berries, as they might copy you and eat something that could make them ill. When foraging in the woods, you must be aware of the potential dangers of handling potentially poisonous plants, fruits and nuts. In the absence of having an expert on hand there are some excellent illustrated books available. Best play safe, though, and make it your rule that if in doubt, don't touch! Never allow children to pick wild mushrooms and toadstools.

'I WANT THE FAIRIES TO COME AND LIVE IN MY HOUSE'
TOBY

'WE MADE THE WATER CLEAN FOR THE FAIRIES TO DRINK'
MAISIE

'I LIKE SQUISHING CLAY WITH MY FINGERS. IT FEELS NICE'
SAUL

The search for the

4

The children's awareness of the environment increases and they

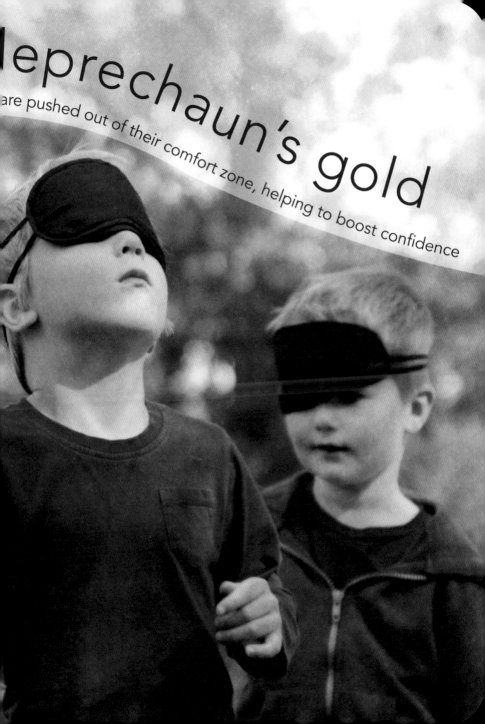

leprechaun's gold

are pushed out of their comfort zone, helping to boost confidence

Telling the story

❛ At the end of the rainbow there is a large crock of gold which is guarded by a small leprechaun. You can recognise him by his grass-green clothes and hat and his carrot-coloured hair and bushy beard.

Finding the start of a rainbow is almost impossible, but there is a trail that will lead us to the crock of gold. It is an invisible way that very few people know about and it can only be followed by those with good listening and looking skills.

We will need to make ourselves journey sticks to remind us where we have been and to help us find our way back without getting lost in the woods. ❜

Setting up the adventure

You will need

Elf bell trail: clear nylon fishing line, hammer, U-shaped nails/ staples, bells, 'handles' made from sticks, ferns, leafy stems

Rainbow trail: coloured yarns in red, orange, yellow, green, blue green, indigo and violet, pot or cauldron, newspaper, gold plastic or chocolate coins, leprechaun costume, eg, a green throw, tall green hat and false ginger beard

Things to make: vegetable peeler, gardening gloves, rubber band, sticky tape

Games to play: blindfolds, hand-held drum

1 Elf bell trail: choose two trees about 5m (15ft) apart. A 'handle' hangs on one tree and is connected by a line running across to the second tree where it is attached to a bunch of bells. The idea being that when a child pulls a handle they hear bells ring and must walk towards the sound. Once they have found the bells, the children look for another handle on a nearby tree farther along the trail. Eventually, they will find their way to the start of the rainbow trail (see page 51). If you can manage it, set up at least three sets of handles and bells.

Nylon fishing line is ideal for this trail as it is strong and the children won't be able see it. Avoid the risk of entanglement by running lines well above adult head height (see Keeping safe on page 57).

On trees with thick, rough bark, such as pines, you can hammer in a U-shaped nail to carry the nylon line. **(a)** On trees with smooth bark, tie a circle of nylon line around the tree trunk and loop the line through that. (See Protecting the woods, page 57.) At the end of the day collect up all the nails and lengths of nylon and dispose of them responsibly.

Tie bells in bunches. **(b)** Make handles from circlets of fern fronds (twist their stems together to stop them springing apart). **(c)** Or use a leafy stem or a small stick. **(d)**

2 Make the rainbow trail: find a secluded area in the woods well away from where the other activities will take place during the day. You don't want to spoil the surprise! Choose at least three trees that are around 3–4.5m (10–15ft) apart. The children will be following the trail blindfolded, so check the ground is level and the surrounding area is free of any trip hazards.

The first colour in the rainbow is red, so tie the end of the ball of red yarn around the tree at the start of the trail. Run the yarn at children's hand height across to the second tree on the trail, pull it taut and wrap it around the trunk. Give it another tug to check it's tight, then run it along to the next tree, repeating the whole process until you have reached the last tree on the trail. Tie off the end of the yarn. Do the same with each of the remaining coloured yarns in the order that they appear in the rainbow (after red comes orange, then yellow, green, blue, indigo and violet). **(e)** Space the individual colours about 2.5cm (1in) apart. (At the end of the day, remember to gather up all the yarns to reuse or dispose of responsibly.)

Have the blindfolds to hand.

3 Crock of gold: before adding the coins, scrunch up the newspaper and use it to pad out the bottom of the crock – that way you won't need so many coins. **(f)** Place the crock near the end of the rainbow but somewhere that still involves a bit of a hunt. Ideally, hang it just out of reach of the children. Pack the leprechaun's outfit in a rucksack and hide it behind a tree close to where you have hidden the crock of gold.

Things to make

☆ **Making journey sticks:** used by Native American Indians when travelling or tracking, journey sticks are a linear map or record of things encountered along a trail. **(g)** Get each child to find a stick that is at least 1ft (30cm) long. (For which woods to choose, see Keeping safe, page 19). They may want to peel away the bark using a vegetable peeler to create some beautiful patterns (see page 14 for how to do it). During the adventure, remind the children to keep adding things to their journey sticks, such as feathers and leaves. This helps them to become aware of their surroundings.

Games to play

☆ **Blindfolded sneaking drum:** this game encourages children to develop skills such as listening, spacial awareness and co-ordination. It is also an important trust exercise. First, give the children blindfolds. **(h)** Tell the children to follow the sound of the drum and that they must stand still when the drum stops. To ensure everyone understands the rules, get the children to have a quick run through first without their blindfolds. Start off by banging the drum from a close distance so they can hear; later you can increase the distance and height to test the listening skills of the children. **(i)** Keep an eye out for trip hazards.

Following the trail

☆ **Following the elf bell trail:** to find the rainbow and the crock of gold the children must follow the elf bell trail. First, they should look for a handle on a tree (you may need to give a description), give it a gentle tug, then follow the sound of the bells to find the next handle on the trail. If they struggle to find the handles use the sound of the drum to draw them close. Or tell them whether they are 'getter hotter' (closer) or 'getting colder' (farther away). When a handle is found, let each child pull it and get them to point to where the sound of the bells is coming from. After the last child has had a go, track down the bells and start looking for the next handle.

☆ **Deer ears game:** listening out for the bells and trying to locate them offers a great opportunity to practise deer ears. Instructions for this game can be found on page 88.

Completing the adventure

☆ **We've found the rainbow!** Line the children up and, one at a time, get them to follow the wool from tree to tree until they reach the end of the rainbow. Pop a blindfold on before they start and make sure they don't rush, placing one hand in front of the other and feeling for any obstacles along the way. Once they have reached the end, whisper for them to take off the blindfold and sit quietly so as not to distract the others. **(j,k)**

☆ **Finding the crock of gold:** once everyone has followed the rainbow trail, slip away to get dressed in your leprechaun's outfit. Get into position with the coin-filled crock next to you. Now the children have to find you – sound a hand-held drum to guide them. Next, get them to line up in front of you and tell them they must take it in turns to sneak up on you while you are snoozing and try to take a piece of gold without waking you up. If you wake and see someone with their hand in the crock they will have to start their approach again. **(l)** Once everyone has a coin, it's time to use the journey sticks to retrace your steps home. Slip out of your costume and join the children, pointing out familiar landmarks on the way.

BEING IN TUNE WITH
YOUR SENSES
INCREASES YOUR
AWARENESS

j

k

l

What did we learn today?

☆ What animals have no sight? If they don't use their eyes, which other senses do they use to find their way around?

☆ What animals have good hearing?

☆ What did it feel like to be blindfolded?

☆ Did the journey sticks help everyone to find their way in the woods?

☆ Why are maps important? Why do we need to know where we are and where we are going?

Keeping safe In this adventure we use nylon fishing line for the elf bell trail. To avoid anyone getting entangled, run the lines between the trees well above adult head height. Warn parents and accompanying adults of the potential risks. Supervise the children at all times. At the end of the day, dismantle the trail and dispose of the nylon line responsibly.

Protecting the woods Please don't fix anything to a young sapling, it has thin bark and you will harm the tree. You must also have permission of the owner of the trees if you want to fix anything to them.

'IT'S DARK WHEN YOU ARE BLINDFOLDED. I CAN HEAR THE WIND'
BETHANY

'I LIKED FOLLOWING THE RAINBOW. WE TUGGED THE LEPRECHAUN'S BEARD'
JOE

'I GOT A HANDFUL OF GOLD COINS. THEY WERE CHOCOLATE'
OLIVIA

5

Magic potions and

Improve their tracking abilities and their knowledge of

wizards' power wands

woodland plants, and push their whittling skills to the next level

Telling the story

❝ *Hidden deep in the woods are three very special ingredients that, when combined together, make a magic potion which can make wishes come true. With the help of this potion and a power wand you can become a wizard. Your special powers can only be used to help people – they won't work if you try to cast naughty spells!*

First, we must find pixie dust. Pixies use it to make themselves invisible. To find our second ingredient, goblin juice, we must follow

the trail of arrows hidden on the forest floor. Troll juice is our third and final ingredient. As well as being the most powerful, it is also the stinkiest and smelliest. To find it we must follow the troll's huge footprints... and be ready to hold our noses! *

Setting up the adventure

You will need

For one bowl of magic potion (see page 66) you will need 150ml (¼ pint) each of troll and green goblin juice, plus 1 tbsp pixie dust (bicarbonate of soda/baking soda)

Troll juice: ½ red cabbage, chopped, lidded pan, 1 litre (2 pints) water, stove, 500ml (1 pint) plastic drinks bottles

Green goblin juice: bottle distilled malt vinegar, 500ml (1 pint) plastic drinks bottles, green food colouring, hessian squares, rubber bands

Laying the trail: flour, bicarbonate of soda (baking soda) decanted into a small tin, sticks for arrows, gardening gloves

Wizards' wands: green wood sticks about 30cm (1ft) long

Things to make: gardening gloves, vegetable peelers, feathers, rubber bands, sticky tape

Completing the adventure: photos or examples of leaves, moss, grass, pine cones, clear plastic bowls, plastic bowls

1 Make troll juice: put the red cabbage in a large pan and cover with the water. Pop on a lid and leave it bubbling away for 20 minutes. **(a)** Allow the liquid to cool before decanting into the plastic drinks bottles. Be warned it smells pretty awful and can stain clothing. When bicarbonate of soda (baking soda) is added to the cabbage water it will change colour from purple to blue. If you have a large group of children you may wish to make multiple bottles.

2 Make green goblin juice: decant 150ml (¼ pint) vinegar into a plastic drinks bottle. Add a few drops of green food colouring and shake to mix. Wrap in hessian and secure with a rubber band. **(b)** Camouflage the bottle with leaf litter, moss and grass.

3 Laying the trail: the trail consists of three different tracks for the children to follow: flour (fairy dust), arrows made from sticks **(c)** ar ¹ large footprints (troll's prints). **(d)**

Hide the tin of pixie dust (bicarbonate of soda/baking soda) in the woods and run a trail of flour back to your starting point. Starting from where the pixie dust is hidden, lay a trail of stick arrows to the hidden bottle/s of vinegar (green goblin juice). Finish the trail by

making giant troll prints – scrape off the top soil. Run the prints across to where you have hidden the troll juice (cabbage water).

Make wands: cut green wood sticks. (See page 19 for which woods are best to use.)

Things to make

☆ **Making power wands:** give each child a short stick. If they want to try bark peeling – it's fun to do and makes lovely decorative patterns – see page 14 for how to do it. **(e)** Decorate the wands with feathers and leaves held in place with rubber bands or sticky tape. **(f)**

☆ **Making a wand stand:** pile pine cones or stones into small mounds. When the children are playing they can plant their wands in the mounds to keep them safe. **(g)**

Games to play

☆ **Grandma's footsteps:** this game teaches children to be quiet and stealthy in the woods and improves their tracking skills. The leader walks ahead of the group and when s/he turns around the children must freeze. If they move or make a noise they have to go to the back of the group. **(h,i)**

Following the trail

☆ **Finding the magic ingredients:** divide the children into groups and let them take turns to find and follow the trail. Before they start, explain why it's important to be quiet when tracking and what is meant by camouflage (they will be looking for the hessian-covered bottles). The trail starts by following the fairy dust (flour). **(j)** Get them to test it's real fairy dust by touching it with their finger – if it tingles it is fairy dust (the power of suggestion usually sets off a tingle). Make sure they don't put it in their mouths. The flour trail will lead them to the container of pixie dust (bicarbonate of soda/baking soda). Next, they must follow the arrows **(k)** to find the green goblin juice (green-coloured vinegar). Young children might not know what an arrow is – make one so they know what to look for. If they are struggling to find the bottles, guide them in by calling out 'getting hotter' (closer) or 'getting colder' (farther away). The last trail follows the troll's prints and leads them to the troll juice (cabbage water). **(l)** Let them have a sniff – it's very pungent.

INCREASING TRACKING SKILLS HELPS THE CHILDREN NOTICE MORE SIGNS OF WILDLIFE

Completing the adventure

☆ **Making the magic potion:** give each child a plastic bowl or bag and some photos or examples of leaves, moss, grass, pine cones, which they could collect to add to the potion. For one bowl of potion, pour 150ml (¼ pint) troll juice (cabbage water) into a container and add 1 tbsp pixie dust (bicarbonate of soda/baking soda). **(l)** Give it a mix and watch it turn from purple to blue. **(m)** Add the collected leaves, etc, and mix well. **(n)** Time to think of a magic spell and a wish – if the potion works, hopefully, it will come true. The final item to add to the mix, is 150ml (¼ pint) green goblin juice (green-coloured vinegar). As the potion fizzes up **(p)** tell the children that all its power is being transferred into their wands. Remind them that they must only be used for good spells!

What did we learn today?

☆ What were the name of the different tracks?

☆ What else leaves tracks in the woods?

☆ What other things do animals and birds leave behind that can be used to track? (eg, feathers, fur and poo)

☆ Why is it important to be quiet when tracking?

☆ Can you remember the ingredients that you found on the forest floor?

Protecting the woods The bicarbonate of soda (baking soda) used in this adventure can kill grass and other plants. When you're mixing up the potions, place the bowls on a sheet of plastic or on a bed of leaf litter, which you can gather up later and dispose of in a bin. If you have a watering can to hand, dilute any splashes with plenty of clean water.

The best way to finish the day Gathered around a fire and enjoying a hot chocolate and freshly made popcorn, children and adults celebrate the day's successes and reflect on what everyone has achieved.

'I LIKED IT WHEN THE MAGIC POTION BUBBLED UP'
LILY

'I MADE A POWER WAND AND IT'S FULL OF WIZARD'S MAGIC'
GARETH

'THE TROLL HAS GOT BIGGER FEET THAN MY DADDY'
CASEY

6

Whoosh! Watch the

Nature's warnings, managing danger and the importance of

rainbow volcanoes fizz

stealth in the woodlands are all covered in this exciting adventure

Telling the story

❝ *Legend has it that at the end of the rainbow there is a large crock of gold. It's hard to see and is guarded by a very small man called a leprechaun. He dresses all in green with a large hat and pointy black shoes. This morning he was hurrying through the woods. He was going so quickly he dropped some of his precious gold. Shall we see if we can find it?*

To track down the gold we will need to pass through the land of the rainbow volcanoes, a place where coloured bubbles shoot out of the ground at any moment. To walk past these volcanoes safely, we must make safety sticks to help warn others, especially the fairies who are scared of them erupting. The fairies have also given us a special magic potion to use to make them safe.

In nature, creatures and plants use bright colours to warn others that they are dangerous, such as yellow and black wasps and the red and white-spotted toadstools you see in fairy stories. **,**

Setting up the adventure

You will need

Rainbow volcanoes: for one volcano – 1 tbsp bicarbonate of soda (baking soda), six drops of food colouring (ideally use a different colour for each volcano), 50ml (1½fl oz) water, plastic measuring jug, 500ml (1 pint) plastic drinks bottle, 150ml (¼ pint) distilled malt vinegar, modelling clay

Laying the trail: hand trowel, gold plastic coins, bag white flour

Super volcanoes: for one volcano – 2 litre (4 pint) bottle fizzy, diet cola, seven chewy mints, 'Geyser Tube' (these are widely available from toy shops or online) or use a 10cm (4in) length of 2cm (¾in) diameter plastic tubing, small lidded tin or tub

Things to make: short, strong stick for each child, feathers, leaves, glitter glues, rubber bands, sticky tape

Completing the adventure: blindfold, water pistol

1 Prepare the rainbow volcanoes: for one rainbow volcano, mix together 1 tbsp bicarbonate of soda (baking soda), add more for a bigger eruption), 50ml (1½fl oz) water and a little food colouring in a jug. Pour into a plastic drinks bottle. Use different food colours to make up more rainbow volcanoes. These don't erupt with a violent explosion, just a delightful fizz of coloured froth.

Fill a second plastic drinks bottle with vinegar (white goblin juice). You will need a quarter of a bottle to trigger the eruption of each rainbow volcano. Wrap the bottle in hessian and secure with rubber bands. Tuck in some moss and leaves as camouflage. The leader can either carry the vinegar around with them or hide it by the first volcano for the children to find.

2 Laying the trail: wearing gardening gloves to protect

your hands, use a hand trowel to dig a small hole in the ground for a rainbow volcano. It should be deep enough so that the top half of the bottle sits clear above soil level. Press a lump of modelling clay around the neck of the bottle to form the top of the volcano. **(a)** Scoop soil, leaf litter and leaves up around the bottle to form a neat mound. Place one leprechaun's gold coin on each mound. Repeat the process for each rainbow volcano along the trail. (Leave the super volcanoes for the end of the trail.)

3 **Prepare the super volcanoes:** bury the super volcanoes (bottles of cola) as for step 2. **(b)** When these erupt they can throw a jet of fizzing bubbles up to 3m (10ft) in the air, so you must set up a safety line for everyone to stand behind. Sprinkle a big circle around the area using white flour (tell the children it's fairy dust).

Place the chewy mints and the Geyser Tube in a lidded tin or tub near the super volcanoes but outside the fairy (safety) ring. Cover over the tin with leaves.

Things to make

☆ **Making safety sticks:** for each child, find a stick that is strong enough to be pushed into the ground. Get them to decorate their sticks with feathers, leaves and glitter glues – the brighter the better. **(c)** Use rubber bands or sticky tape to attach the decorations. The children will use their safety sticks to mark the positions of the volcanoes along the trail. **(d)**

Games to play

☆ **The colours game:** this game will help children link colours with the natural environment. Gather them into a group and get them to sit quietly on the floor. Ask them to close their eyes and listen carefully to your instructions. When they hear the name of a colour they have to find something in the woods that is the same colour. They can either jump up and collect an item that matches the colour – speed, of course, will be of the essence – or they can stay seated and count on their fingers how many things they can see. If they can name the coloured objects, so much the better. Be ready with a vocabulary prompt.

Following the trail

☆ **Looking for the volcanoes:** don't assume the children will know what a volcano looks like – an explanation may be needed. You may want to divide the children into small groups for this activity. Tell everyone that they are looking for the gold coins that have been dropped by a leprechaun. **(e,f)** If a second group is following behind, tell the children to leave the coins where they found them. Once a volcano has been found mark its position with a safety stick to warn people and fairies of the danger of an imminent eruption.

Take this opportunity to teach tracking skills. Tell everyone to be quiet and walk without scuffing their feet or snapping twigs underfoot so as not to disturb the fairies or wild creatures. Show them examples of tracks they might find in the woods and discuss which creatures made them.

Completing the adventure

☆ **Erupting the rainbow volcanoes:** nominate one child to pour in a quarter of the bottle of white goblin juice (vinegar) into the top of the volcano. The rest of group can be chanting a spell, such as 'Abracadabra volcano safe!' Everyone stand back, then, after a few seconds, watch the coloured bubbles erupt. Mark the spot with a safety stick so the fairies will know there is a volcano in the area. Now let's go find the next one!

☆ **Erupting the super volcanoes:** after all the rainbow volcanoes have erupted, tell the children that because they have done such a good job making them safe you now need them to do the same with some super volcanoes. To find them they must look for the circle of fairy dust (flour). Inside are the volcanoes which they must mark with safety sticks.

To launch the super volcanoes the children must acquire one more ingredient – a magic pellet (chewy mint) – which is guarded by a sleeping elf (an adult wearing a blindfold). The children must sneak past the elf and grab a magic pellet from the tin. If the elf wakes s/he will try to squirt them with a water pistol. Once all the children have a magic pellet (chewy mint) their spell is repeated with the word 'super' added, 'Abracadabra super volcano safe!'.

Check that everyone is back behind the safety line, then *discreetly* take the top off the cola bottle and tell everyone to listen out for the sound of escaping volcanic gasses (bubbles fizzing). Get the children to drop their mints into the Geyser Tube. Then, following pack instructions, screw the Geyser Tube on to the bottle and pull out the clip allowing the mints to drop into the drink. Quickly move back outside the fairy ring to watch the jet of foam shoot up to 3m (10ft) in the air. **(g)**

Hooray! The children have successfully made all the volcanoes safe for the fairies and marked their position just in case they become active again in the future. On the return journey, get the children to collect up the gold pieces along the way. At the end of the day, retrieve the plastic bottles and safety sticks and tidy up the play area, see page 81.

THIS ADVENTURE HAS LOTS OF GREAT LEARNING POINTS FOR THE CHILDREN

What did we learn today?

☆ What is a volcano?

☆ How many volcanoes did we find today?

☆ Who can remember the different colours of the volcanoes?

☆ What were the safety sticks for? Do we know of any other signs in nature that warn us of danger?

☆ What are tracks and who might leave them in the woods?

☆ What tracks do we make?

☆ Why is it good to walk quietly in the woods?

☆ Will we be able to see more wildlife if we are quiet or noisy?

Protect the woods The bicarbonate of soda (baking soda) used in the rainbow volcanoes will kill grass and other plants. Gather up the leaf litter in the area and dispose of it in a bin. If you have a watering can to hand, dilute any splashes with plenty of clean water.

whoosh! watch the rainbow volcanoes fizz

'THE GREEN RAINBOW VOLCANO WAS MY FAVOURITE'
GABI

'THE SUPER VOLCANO WENT RIGHT UP INTO THE SKY'
GEORGE

'MY SAFETY STICK WILL KEEP THE FAIRIES SAFE'
EMILY

are letting off
rockets

improve knowledge of plants and marvel at the mysteries of flight

Telling the story

❝ Does anyone know who helps Father Christmas make his toys? Yes, it's the elves. But elves don't only live in the North Pole, they have relatives all over the world. There are some of their cousins, the wood elves, living in these woods. Every year, the elf families gather in the North Pole for a huge party and the wood elves make the long journey in super-charged rockets.

Would you like to know how the elves make their special rockets? You do! Then we must gather the magic ingredients which are hidden among the trees. ❞

Setting up the adventure

You will need

Launch pad: drill, wood plank 300 x 200mm (2ft x 8in), 80mm (3in) long screw, cork (to fit snugly in the top of a 500ml (1 pint) plastic drinks bottle)

Potions: to make one rocket – 150ml (¼ pint) malt vinegar, 60ml (2fl oz) water with a few drops of green food colouring added, 1 tbsp bicarbonate of soda (baking soda) and three 500ml (1 pint) clear plastic drinks bottles, hessian squares, rubber bands

Launch site: bag white flour

Things to make: 500ml (1pint) clear plastic drinks bottles (one per rocket launch), rubber bands, sticky tape

Games to play: hand-held drum

Completing the adventure: plastic cups, examples or photos of leaves, moss, grass and pine cones (optional)

1 Make the launch pad: drill a hole (slightly smaller than the screw) in the middle of the plank of wood, drive in the screw, then twist the cork on to the screw until it fits tight against the wood. **(a)** The plank doesn't have to be an exact size, just large enough to hold the rocket steady.

2 Prepare the potions: use one bottle each for the vinegar (brown goblin juice), green coloured water (elf juice) and the bicarbonate of soda (baking soda/pixie dust). Wrap in hessian and secure with rubber bands. **(b)** Camouflage with leaves, moss and grass.

3 Laying the trail: hide the bottles in the woods, **(c)** then lay a trail of stick arrows so the children can find them. Change the size and shape of the arrows to increase the difficulty. **(d)**

4 Choose a launch site: mark out a safety line with a sprinkling of flour (fairy dust) well back from the launch pad. NB: when you have finished the adventure you will need to tidy up the site, see page 81.

e

f

Things to make

☆ **Making elf rockets:** 500ml (1 pint) plastic drinks bottles are an ideal size for the rockets. Check that the top of the bottles fit snugly around the cork on the launch pad. To make the rockets suitable for the wood elves, the children can decorate the bottles with moss, grasses and leaves (avoid using twigs and sticks). Attach the decorations with rubber bands or sticky tape. **(e)** Note, if the decorations are too heavy the rocket won't fly as high. Tell the children not to put anything inside the rocket.

Games to play

☆ **Deer ears game:** the American outdoor-educator Joseph Cornell devised this simple but effective game to increase children's awareness of the different sounds in the woodlands. The children start by cupping their hands and placing them around their ears, palms facing forwards. **(f)** The group leader or a child hides somewhere in the woods away from the others. When they are hidden they sound a drum which the other children on hearing have to search for. Increase the difficulty by decreasing the amount of drumming.

☆ **Deer ear variations:** deer ears can be reversed, with cupped hands placed around the ears, palms facing backwards – this direction is great for hearing anyone or any creature creeping up behind you. This fun game always goes down well with children: a child (the listener) faces away from the group and gets into position with reversed deer ears. The other children take it in turn to creep up behind them to tap them on their shoulder or pick up an object on the floor behind them. If the listener hears someone s/he turns around or puts up a hand to signal for them to go to the back of the group and try again.

Following the trail

☆ **Following the arrows:** these will lead the children to the different magical ingredients they need to make their elf rockets fly **(g,h)** – these are brown goblin juice (vinegar), elf juice (green-coloured water) and pixie dust (bicarbonate of soda/baking soda). If the children are either unfamiliar with arrows or are struggling to find them, run ahead of the group and quickly sprinkle them with some white flour – a little fairy dust should make all the difference!

watch out! the elves are letting off rockets

i

j

k

l

m

Completing the adventure

☆ **Making rocket fuel:** give each child or group a plastic cup. They could collect a leaf, some grass, moss and a pine cone. Show them examples or, if you're really organised, some photos. This task will help develop their identification skills. **(i)** Once they have collected all the items, add the magic ingredients: into each cup, pour 150ml (¼ pint) brown goblin juice (vinegar) and 60ml (2fl oz) elf juice (green-coloured water). This will make enough fuel for one rocket launch. **(j)** Get the children to mix it with a stick, then help them to strain off the liquid into a decorated elf rocket (the 500ml (1 pint) plastic bottle). Cast a magic spell or two, such as 'Abracadabra fly rocket fly'.

☆ **Launching the rocket:** move everyone back behind the safety line. As rockets can shoot up to 10m (30ft) into the air, check the launch site for overhanging trees. Ask the children to think about what can affect the flight of their rocket, eg, the weight of the decorations and the wind direction. Get them to check the wind direction by dropping a few blades of grass from head height and seeing where they fall. Are they up or down wind?

Wrap 1 tbsp pixie dust (bicarbonate of soda/baking soda) in kitchen paper, use single ply, and form a small ball. **(k)** Push the ball into the top of the rocket but not all the way down. **(l)** Press the cork on the launch pad into the top of the rocket to seal it. Invert the bottle and shake it a couple of times. Place the launch pad on level ground making sure it is standing upright. Be careful as the rocket may blast off after a few seconds! **(m)**

What have we learned today?

☆ Where do the elves go in winter?
☆ Where can you travel in a rocket?
☆ What can affect the flight of the rocket?
☆ How do you test wind direction?
☆ Did you stand up wind or down wind from the launch pad?

watch out! the elves are letting off rockets

8

play hide and seek with

Exploring camouflage skills, understanding its importance wher

Sammy the grouse

tracking wildlife and how animals and birds use it to survive

Telling the story

❛ Most birds and animals are good at hide and seek, but there is a small brown bird called a grouse who gets top marks for being hard to find. Grouse are masters of camouflage – their brown stripy feathers make them really hard to see, in fact, you could almost say they were invisible. When you are out walking in the country, if you surprise a grouse who has been hiding it will suddenly fly up into the air and let out a shrill shriek. [Do your best bird impression here!] If you are really quiet, you might be able to sneak up on a grouse and tip it out of its bed.

In these woods there is a grouse called Sammy. He's such a lazy bird, his favourite thing to do is snoozing. You can often hear him snoring which makes him easy to find [demonstrate snoring]. Can you hear him snoring? There is a special machine that will tip him out of bed and teach him to fly off when people are approaching his nest. Shall we go and find him? ❜

play hide and seek with sammy the grouse

95

Setting up the adventure

You will need

Camouflage suits: hessian – each child will need a 100 x 50cm (3ft 3in x 1ft 7in) piece, scissors, string

Rocket valve: unused cork, sharp kitchen knife, drill with 5mm drill bit, old bicycle inner tube, track/foot pump

Toy bird: toy bird (if you can't find a suitable child's toy use a dog toy instead, but please refer to the warning on page 102), 500ml (1 pint) plastic drinks bottle, needle and thread or safety pins

Laying the trail: short lengths of coloured yarns (must include leaf green and dark brown), Velcro strips (hook side only), birds' feathers

Things to make: wooden clothes pegs (optional)

1 **Make camouflage suits:** cut the hessian into rectangles about 100 x 50cm (3ft 3in x1ft 7in). **(a)** Make a circular hole large enough for a child's head in the middle. For optional belts, cut lengths of string.

2 **Make the rocket valve:** cut the cork in half using a sharp knife and drill a 5mm hole vertically through the centre. Check the cork fits the top of a 500ml (1 pint) plastic drinks bottle. Cut the valve out of the inner tube leaving a skirt of rubber. Push the valve into the cork – the rubber skirt will prevent the valve being pushed in too far. **(b)** You may need to trim the cork back a little to expose the threads of the valve. Attach the valve to the pump and test to see if air pushes through freely. **(c)**

3 **Prepare the toy bird:** using sharp scissors, unpick the stitching around the bird's bottom. Make the hole large enough to push in the 500ml (1 pint) plastic drinks bottle. Pull out some stuffing so you can push the bottle inside with its top just poking out. Repack the stuffing around the bottle. Sew or safety pin the fabric together around the top of the bottle.

Carefully pour 100ml (3fl oz)

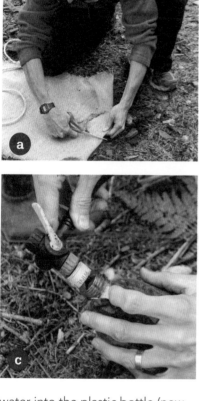

water into the plastic bottle (now inside the bird) and push in the cork. Attach the pump. Make a shallow scrape on the ground as a nest in the bracken for Sammy. Set him at a slight angle with his head up. **(d)** Stand the pump on a flat piece of ground nearby. Cover over the hose with leaves and soil.

4 **Laying the trails:** scatter lengths of coloured yarn (caterpillars) over an area of a few metres. Lay a trail of feathers to Sammy's hidden nest.

Things to make

☆ **Making camouflage outfits:** don't assume the children will know what 'camouflage' is, show them examples, such as a green caterpillar on a green leaf, a brown feather on the floor. Explain that their camouflage outfits will help them to blend in with the woods so they can't be seen.

Give each child a hessian rectangle. Check that the neck hole is big enough before they start adding camouflage, eg, leaves, twigs, moss, grass, feathers, bracken. Show them how to thread leaf stems and twigs through the open weave of the hessian. **(e)** They can attach larger items with wooden clothes pegs. Help the children to pull on their tops poncho-style. **(g)** For an optional belt, tie a length of string around their waists.

Games to play

☆ **Find the wiggly caterpillars:** each child is given a piece of Velcro (hook side only and told to look for caterpillars (lengths of coloured yarn). Each time they find one, get them to stick it on to the Velcro. **(f)** At the end of the game get them to think about which coloured caterpillars were

easiest to find and which ones were the most difficult (the natural colours). This is a good way to demonstrate to the children how certain colours are best for camouflage.

☆ **Hide and seek:** this is the perfect game for testing out those new camouflage outfits. Before everyone heads off into the woods, check they remember their adventure call! (See page 7.)

Following the trail

☆ **Finding Sammy the grouse:** to find where Sammy is hiding in his nest they should follow the trail of feathers. Tell everyone to listen out for his snoring. **(h,i)**

Completing the adventure

☆ **Making Sammy fly:** remind the children to be quiet so they will be able to hear Sammy snore. Let them take turns operating the pump, giving it one pump per turn. **(j)** After a few pumps Sammy will be snoring away nicely – it's the sound of air and water bubbling in the bottle. Keep pumping until Sammy flies up out of his nest. **(k)** His sudden flight will take everyone by surprise, especially as he can fly up to 6m (20ft) in the air. (See Keeping safe on page 103.) If you have time, let each child launch Sammy by themselves. You will need to top up the water level in the bottle after every flight.

What did we learn today?

☆ Why are some insects, animals and birds camouflaged?

☆ Can you think of any creature that uses camouflage? (Some animals, such as the chameleon, can change the colour of their skin to match their surroundings making them hard to see.)

☆ Some insects are very brightly coloured and are easy to see. Why do you think this might be?

Keeping safe Always read the care labels on toys. The bird toy used in this adventure was intended for dogs to chew not young children to play with. Don't allow Sammy the grouse to be picked up by the children, explain that he is a wild bird who doesn't like being cuddled.

When launching the bird into the air a certain amount of high-pressure water spray is released, so keep everyone well back from the launch site or they could get a soaking. When positioning Sammy in his nest, make sure he's facing away from the person operating the pump!

'I COULD HEAR SAMMY SNORING IN HIS BED'
BELLA

'NO ONE COULD SEE ME IN MY LEAF SUIT. I HID IN THE WOODS'
ROXY

'I MADE SAMMY THE GROUSE FLY UP INTO THE AIR'
JAMES

9

Help wake up the

Magical skills will be needed, plus an increased awareness of

sleeping stick wizards

the senses and an indepth knowledge of woodland wildlife

Telling the story

❝ Before the old stick wizard woke up the sticks in the wood, a terrible rot had set in. Most days the sticks just lay down and slept or propped themselves lazily against a tree letting the mould grow on their toes. But the old stick wizard is looking forward to his retirement and is hoping to recruit some younger stick wizards to take over the care of the woodlands for him.

The new stick wizards will have to be brave and good at skills such as tracking, finding things, running fast, potion making, spell casting and talking with all the creatures and plants in the woods. Would you like to make the new stick men and train them to be strong and wise? ❞

Setting up the adventure

You will need

Magic potions trail: 200g (7oz) bicarbonate of soda (baking soda), 500ml (1 pint) distilled malt vinegar, 500ml (1 pint) red cabbage juice (for how to make it, see page 62), three 500ml (1pint) clear plastic drinks bottles, hessian squares, rubber bands, small bells

Animal trail: soft toys such as a squirrel, bird, fox, snake, clear nylon fishing line, acorns, beech or monkey nuts, feathers, sturdy stick

Stick wizard: set of googly eyes (from craft shops) and sticks (one per child and one for your stick wizard), modelling clay

Completing the adventure: plastic cauldron or black bucket

The trail is set out in the same way as the Elf bell trail, on page 48. On one tree you hang a 'handle' which is connected by nylon line to bells hanging on another tree. The trail comprises three pairs of trees – one with a handle on it, one with bells. Hide one ingredients bottle at the base of each bell tree.

1 Laying the magic potions trail: decant the three ingredients – bicarbonate of soda (baking soda), vinegar and cabbage juice – into separate plastic drinks bottles. Wrap each of the bottles in hessian secured with rubber bands.

2 Laying the animal trail: decide where each of the stuffed toys is going to be hidden. The squirrel and bird can be sitting on a low perch, while the fox and snake can be tucked into suitably

snug hideaways on the ground.

Next, lay an appropriate trail for the children to follow to each of the creatures. For example, if you are using a squirrel toy, lay a trail of acorns, beech or monkey nuts. For a bird toy, sprinkle a trail of feathers. For a snake toy, use a stick to draw a series of wiggly lines on the ground. You may need to go over the lines several times so they are clearly visible.

3 **Animating the toys:** tie a length of nylon line to each toy and loop it over a convenient branch above head height (to avoid any risk of entanglement). On trees with rough bark you can use U-shaped nails (see Elf bell trail on page 48). Attach the end of the line to a stick. During the adventure give the line a discreet tug to make the creatures move, eg, the bird to fly up into the tree.

4 **Make a stick wizard:** for how to, see Things to make on page 110. Once you have finished making your wizard, hide him in the woods next to the starting point of the magic potions trail.

Things to make

☆ **Making stick wizards:** each child will need a stick and two lumps of modelling clay, one to form a head and one for a body, plus a pair of googly eyes. For arms, legs, hair and facial features get them to use items they collect in the woods. For inspiration, let them see the stick wizards in this book or make up your own stick wizard to show them how to do it. **(d,e)**

Games to play

☆ **Animal impressions:** this game gets children to think about what different animals look like, how they sound and how they move. Get everyone slowly marching along, then shout out the name of an animal. The children must do an impression of that animal on the spot, paying attention to noises, movement and speed. For example, a squirrel will scamper away really quickly and hide. **(f)**

d

e

Following the trail

☆ **Finding the animals:** the children must introduce their stick wizards to the animals in the woodland. Remind them to be quiet or the creatures will be frightened and fly or run away. When they approach the hideaways of the squirrel and the bird, pull on the nylon lines to make them race up into the tree. As the children gradually settle, you can lower the toys so they can introduce their stick wizards. Be ready to pull them up again if the children try to reach out and touch them. Remind everyone that wild creatures aren't pets and don't like to be handled. Note that toys, such as the fox and snake, are raised up from their hideaways to meet the children. If things get too boisterous, lower them out of sight rather than yanking them up! **(g,h)** Explain why it's not safe to handle a snake or a fox.

Discuss with the children where different creatures live, eg, birds nest in trees, foxes prefer a hole in the ground, and what they like to eat.

☆ **Finding the magic potion:** once the children's stick wizards have been introduced to the woodland creatures, it's time to take them along to meet the old stick wizard who will help them complete their training. But first they must find the ingredients to make the magic potion. See if they can spot the 'handle' on the stick wizard's tree. Let the children take turns pulling the handle to set the bells ringing. Get them to point in the direction of the sound. If they need help finding the bells, prompt them with 'getting hotter' (closer) or 'getting colder' (farther away). Near the 'bell' tree they will find an ingredients bottle. They must find a second 'handle' and repeat the process until they have all three ingredients.

Completing the adventure

☆ **Making the magic potion:** pour the troll juice (cabbage water) into the cauldron, then add the pixie dust (bicarbonate of soda/baking soda). **(i)** Let each child take a turn stirring – the purple solution will turn blue. **(j)** Add the white goblin juice (vinegar), say your best magic spells and the potion will start to bubble. **(k,l)** The new stick wizards are ready to take care of the forest.

TEAMWORK MAKES FOR BETTER POTIONS AND POWERFUL MAGIC SPELLS!

What did we learn today?

☆ How can you get close to the creatures who live in the woods?

☆ Is it okay for us to try to stroke wild animals and birds?

☆ Why might an animal try to bite you? Do you think it could be because they are scared?

☆ Why is it important to look after the woodland and how best can we do that?

☆ Before we head home why should we tidy up our play area?

Keeping safe Nylon fishing line is used in this adventure. Be aware that there is a risk of entanglement both to humans and wildlife. For tips on how to use it safely around children, please refer to Keeping safe, on page 57. Remember to collect up any line at the end of the day and dispose of it responsibly.

Protecting the woods Please refrain from fixing anything to young saplings, especially nylon line, as their bark is thin and easily damaged. Never hammer metal fixings into the bark of a tree as it causes harm.

When using bicarbonate of soda (baking soda) in this adventure lay down a sheet of plastic first or spread a bed of leaf litter which can be gathered up and disposed of in a bin. Dilute any spills with water.

'I LOVE MY STICK WIZARD. HE'S COMING HOME WITH ME' JASMINDA

'I HEARD THE SNAKE GO SHHHH SHHHH!' TOM

'THE ANIMALS AND THE BIRDS WANT US TO KEEP THEIR HOME TIDY' TULISA

help wake up the sleeping stick wizards

10

The lost treasure of

Reading a compass and following bearings are advanced

the woodland pirates

skills made simple in this exciting quest to find the pirates' treasure

Telling the story

❝ *Once upon a time, where we are standing now, was part of a large river which led to the sea. One day, a band of pirates sailed down it, their boat laden with treasure from far-off lands. Suddenly, they were caught in a big storm and they started to sink. The only way for their boat to stay afloat was to unload the treasure. The pirates took it into the woods and buried it, marking the spot with a large X so they could find it again. Then they jumped back aboard their boat and sailed away.*

Many years later the pirates returned but they could not find their treasure. They vowed never to return to sea until it was found – but they searched and searched the woods until they grew into old men with long white beards. But they never found their treasure. This is how they became known as the woodland pirates.

There is a place they didn't look, hidden deep in the woods. Shall we see if we can find the pirates' lost treasure? "

Setting up the adventure

You will need

Bury the treasure: treasure chest, tin or box, gold/silver plastic coins, hand trowel, two sticks

Card compass: four A4 pieces of card (one each of red, yellow, blue and green, ideally laminated), waterproof marker pen, sheet of plastic or board, an arrow cut out of white card, real compass

Flag markers: two different coloured plastic bags, scissors, sticky tape, 30cm (1ft) green split bamboo plant sticks

Things to make: cardboard tubes from kitchen rolls, rubber bands

Completing the adventure: children's spades, water pistol

1 **Bury the treasure:** fill the pirates' chest with coins, then dig a hole and bury it. **(a)** Cover it over and mark the spot with a large X using two sticks. **(b)**

2 **Make the card compass:** cut each sheet of coloured card into quarters. Label all the red rectangles with an N – on most

compasses red is the colour of the needle that points North. Label the yellow pieces with a W, the green with an E and the blue with an S. On a piece of stiff clear plastic or board, stick down a card for each compass point. **(c)** Don't stick the white arrow down.

3 **Laying the trail:** using just the four main compass points (N, S, E and W), lay a trail for the children to follow. Try this very simple routing:

With the buried treasure as the end point of your trail, find North on the compass. (See How to use

a compass, right.) Turn to face South, ie, away from the direction the red needle is pointing, and walk a short distance in a straight line. Scatter the red cards on the floor. Use the compass again, find where E is and walk towards it in a straight line. At a convenient point, drop the yellow cards. Refer to the compass again and head North. Drop the blue cards. Head West, making sure you go beyond where the treasure is buried before you drop the green cards. Finally, head South to determine where the starting point of the trail will be. Note, the children will follow the trail in the opposite direction to the way you have just walked it.

How to use a compass: if you've never used a compass before here's how. Hold the compass flat in your hand so the needle is free to move. Turn the compass around until the red pointer lines up with the letter N on the dial. To go North you follow the direction of the red pointer.

4 Make flag markers: you will need two different coloured flags. Cut two flag shapes from each plastic bag. Fix each to the top of a plant stick with sticky tape.

the lost treasure of the woodland pirates

Things to make

☆ **Making telescopes:** draw a line around the bottom few inches of each cardboard tube. Get the children to decorate the tubes with leaves and grasses, holding everything in place with rubber bands and sticky tape. **(d,e)** Below the line keep the tube bare of decoration to avoid eye injuries.

Explain what a telescope is and what magnification is. Get them to imagine how the pirates used their telescopes at sea to check the horizon for ships or land. How will they use their telescopes in the woods? See if they can spot a bird in the top of a tree? Can they see the buried treasure?

Games to play

☆ **Finding the flag:** this games helps children increase their awareness of their environment, to work in teams and burn off excess energy. Hide the

two flags in the woods (make sure they are well away from the treasure trail). Divide the group into two teams and give each a name, say Robins and Wrens (make it birds they may actually see in the woods), and designate two trees as their home bases. After you've shouted 'ready, steady, go!', the children must run off to find a flag. As soon as a child locates it, **(f,g)** they must run back to their home tree, calling their team mates back, too, by shouting, 'Robins go home!'. To make the game more challenging, hide the flags and use a compass bearing to tell the groups which direction to run. (They will need to refer to the card compass to guide them.)

This variation makes good use of the children's telescopes. Position the flags somewhere in sight but not obvious so that they need to concentrate in order to find them. Once they have located their flag they must run over to collect it and bring it back to their tree.

Following the trail

☆ **Finding the treasure:** show the children the red needle on the real compass and ask them to point in the direction that it points. Tell them that is North. Place the compass in the middle of the card compass and turn it so the red card N is in North position. Get the children to position the white card arrow so it faces North. **(h)** Now they are ready to follow the treasure trail North. Taking both compasses with you: hold the real one in your hand and let the children check that they are walking in the right direction. **(i)** When they find the green cards, show them on the card compass that this means they should next walk East. Keep walking and checking the compass until they find the blue cards. Keep following the trail around until you find the buried treasure. X marks the spot. Start digging! **(j)**

Completing the adventure

☆ **Sharing out the treasure:** let the children relish the moment they open the treasure chest and find it full of gold and silver coins. **(k)**

☆ **Guarding the treasure:** once everyone has had a chance to play with the coins, warn them they must watch out for the pirates in case they come back to claim their treasure. The children can each take it in turn to stand guard with a water pistol while other members of the group try to sneak up and grab a coin. If someone gets squirted, they must start their approach again.

What did we learn today?

☆ Can you remember the names of all the points on the compass?

☆ Which direction does the red needle on the compass point?

☆ When would you use a compass?

☆ If you get lost in the woods what should you do? (Call out for help and use your adventure call, see page 7.)

Index

index

Acknowledgments

Writing this book has been an adventure in itself – a huge collaborative one. I would like to thank all the children who came along to be photographed, as well as their families for allowing them to do so. Their enthusiasm and patience was a great source of inspiration. Particular thanks to Jen, Pete, Oliver and Charlie Todman, Colin, Liz and Bethany Snowball and Gareth Ayres. Thanks also to Jollydays Glamping for allowing us to use their magical woodlands.

Thank you to the following companies and people who consented to the use of their products: Wild Republic Toys, Nemesis Now, Penfound Products, David Lawrence, Bristol Novelty, Living Nature, Camping Solutions and House of Paws.

A special thanks to my wife Marie for her eagle eyes when reading through my copy and for listening to me rambling on about leprechauns and fairies.

Finally, a big thank you to Frances Lincoln for this amazing opportunity to turn a dream into a reality.

Additional resources

Publications
I Love My World by Chris Holland (Wholeland), *Sharing Nature with Children* by Joseph Cornell (Dawn Publications), *Run Wild!* by Jo Schofield and Fiona Danks (Frances Lincoln)

Organisations
www.forestschoolassociation.org, www.forestschools.com, www.forestry.gov.uk/england, www.woodlandtrust.org.uk, www.bushbabies-woodlandadventures.co.uk

acknowledgments